Mostly blue

Blue-gray Gnatcatcher
blue gray with dark forehead

Cerulean Warbler
white chin, thin breast band, female duller

Indigo Bunting
blue with dark wings

female brown

male

Tree Swallow
white chin and chest

Eastern Bluebird
sky blue with rusty chest, female duller

Barn Swallow
orange forehead, forked tail, female duller

Blue Grosbeak
rusty wing bars

female brown

male

female

Purple Martin
nearly black, notched tail, female gray belly

male

T0123827

4"
7"
8 1/2"

Blue Jay

blue crest,
black necklace

Belted Kingfisher

shaggy crest,
female has
two bands
on chest

Mostly yellow

Blue-winged Warbler

yellow cap,
black eye line,
dark eyes,
female duller

Nashville
Warbler

gray head,
yellow throat
and chest

American
Goldfinch

male

black forehead,
female lacks
black forehead

American Redstart

yellow patches,
white belly

male orange

female

12" 13" 4 1/2" 4 3/4" 5" 5"

Brown Creeper

long curved bill

House Finch

brown cap, streaked flanks and belly

male red

female

Pine Siskin

yellow streaks on wings, female less yellow

Common Redpoll

red cap, red wash on chest, female lacks red wash

Chipping Sparrow

rusty cap, clear chest

House Wren

short curved bill

Chimney Swift

pointed head and tail as seen in flight

Chestnut-sided Warbler

yellow cap, chestnut sides, female duller

5"   5"   5"   5"   5"   5"   5"   5"

Mostly brown

Bank Swallow
white throat and belly, dark breast band

Cliff Swallow
tan-to-rust forehead and cheeks

Northern Rough-winged Swallow
plain brown with gray belly

Dark-eyed Junco
brown with white belly

male gray

female

Indigo Bunting
brown with lighter throat

male blue

female

Carolina Wren
white eyebrows, white markings on sides of neck

Song Sparrow
central dark spot on streaked chest

Field Sparrow
gray and rust head, pink bill

5 1/4"   5 1/2"   5 1/2"   5 1/2"   5 1/2"   5 1/2"   5 1/2"   5 1/2"

Purple Finch

white eye stripe

male red

female

Ovenbird

heavily marked
white chest,
dark stripes on
head

Hermit Thrush

dark spots on
chest, rusty tail

Louisiana Waterthrush

heavily
streaked
chest, white
eyebrows

American Tree Sparrow

rusty cap, central
dark spot on
clear chest

female

House Sparrow

black throat, gray
cap, female tan
eyebrows

male

White-throated Sparrow

white chin,
bold eyebrows

White-crowned Sparrow

black and
white head

6"   6"   6"   6"   6"   6"   6 1/2"   7"

Mostly brown

Fox Sparrow

heavily streaked chest and belly

Swainson's Thrush

brown spots on chin, chest and belly

Blue Grosbeak

brown with tan wing bars

male blue

female

Rose-breasted Grosbeak

bold white eyebrows

female

male black & white

Brown-headed Cowbird

whitish throat

male black

female

Horned Lark

white-to-yellow throat, black necklace, female duller

Eastern Towhee

rusty sides, red eyes

male black

female

Cedar Waxwing

black mask, red wing tips

Wood Thrush

rusty head, black spots on chest and belly

Bohemian Waxwing

black mask, white and red wing tips

7"   7"   7"   7 1/2" 7 1/2" 7 1/2" 7 1/2" 7 1/2" 8" 8 1/4"

Northern Cardinal
black mask, red bill

male red

female

Red-winged Blackbird
light eyebrows

male black

female

Common Nighthawk

white chin, white band across wings as seen in flight, female tan chin

Northern Bobwhite

white eyebrows and chin, female tan eyebrows and chin

Whip-poor-will

large dark eyes, gray on back

Killdeer

two black bands around neck

Brown Thrasher
long tail, long curved bill

Yellow-billed Cuckoo

white chin, dark bars on long tail

8 1/2" 8 1/2" 9" 10" 10" 11" 11" 12"

Mourning Dove

blue eye-ring, bobs head while walking

Northern Flicker

yellow wing linings, black mark on face, female lacks black mark

Boat-tailed Grackle

brown head, long tail, yellow eyes

male black

female

Spruce Grouse

red skin above eyes, female lacks red skin

Ruffed Grouse

dark ruffs

Great-tailed Grackle

long tail, white eyes

female

male black

female

Ring-necked Pheasant

long tail, white ring around neck, female all brown

female

male

Wild Turkey

bare skin on head, black beard, female lacks beard

male

12"   12"   15"   16"   17 1/2"   18"   33"   42"

Mostly black

Bobolink

yellow nape, white shoulders and rump

female yellow

male

Brown-headed Cowbird

brown head, gray bill

male

female brown

European Starling

bill yellow in summer, gray in winter

Eastern Towhee

black head and chest, red eyes

female brown

male

Red-winged Blackbird

red and yellow shoulder patches

female brown

male

Common Grackle

blue head, long tail, female shorter tail

Boat-tailed Grackle

very long tail, yellow eyes

female brown

male

Fish Crow

black with nasal "cah" call

7" 7 1/2" 7 1/2" 7 1/2" 8 1/2" 12" 15" 16"

American Crow
black with familiar "caw" call

Great-tailed Grackle
purple head, long tail, yellow eyes

female brown

male

Common Raven
shaggy throat feathers

Mostly green

Ruby-throated Hummingbird
ruby throat, female lacks ruby throat

18"   18"   24 1/2"   3 1/4"